WEBTOON

LEARN TO DRAW HOOKY

Walter Foster

Quarto.com

This library edition published in 2025 by Walter Foster Publishing, an imprint of The Quarto Group.
100 Cummings Center, Suite 265-D, Beverly, MA 01915, USA.
T (978) 282-9590 F (978) 283-2742

Distributed in the United States and Canada by Lerner Publisher Services
241 First Avenue North
Minneapolis, MN 55401 U.S.A.
www.lernerbooks.com

First Library Edition

Library of Congress Cataloging-in-Publication Control Number: 2024939983

Layout and editorial: Coffee Cup Creative LLC
WEBTOON Rights and Licensing Manager: Amanda Chen
Illustrations and art: Míriam Bonastre Tur and WEBTOON Entertainment, except Shutterstock on pages 32 and 33

This Lerner edition has been edited for content.

Printed in China
10 9 8 7 6 5 4 3 2 1

ISBN: 978-0-7603-9837-1

CONTENTS

INTRODUCTION

Siblings Dani and Dorian are on a quest to harness their magical powers for good.

Grab your enchanted broomstick, a pencil, and some paper and come along on a magical drawing adventure!

WHAT IS HOOKY?

Dani and Dorian Wytte have missed the bus to magic school, so they find a mentor who can teach them everything they need to know. Amid a series of mishaps, the pair discover a plot that spells trouble for the King. Will these siblings be able to learn magic and bring the kingdom together before anyone gets hurt?

Check out all the episodes of the hit WEBTOON series.

SYNOPSIS

In a world where the peace between magic users and non-magic users is tenuous at best, two young witches must learn the hard way that sometimes simple mistakes can have catastrophic consequences!

When twins Dani and Dorian Wytte accidentally missed the bus to magic school, they thought finding their own teacher would be the easy solution. Instead, it wound up leading them down a path that would leave both of them changed forever.

Now, Dani and Dorian need to learn to control their magical abilities and stand up to the mysterious forces threatening to plunge the world into chaos, all while navigating the complicated story of their family.

WHAT IS A WEBCOMIC?

Webcomics are comics published on a website or mobile app.

Meet WEBTOON™.

We started a whole new way to create stories and opened it up to anyone with a story to tell. We're home to thousands of creator-owned series with amazing, diverse visions from all over the world. Get in on the latest original romance, comedy, action, fantasy, horror, and more from big names and big-names-to-be—made just for WEBTOON. We're available anywhere, anytime, and always for free.

FROM THE CREATOR

What inspired you to create Hooky?

My main inspirations were the cartoons, comics, and books I enjoyed as a kid and young teenager. I've always been into fantasy—I still am—so creating my own fantasy story was natural for me. My most obvious inspirations are Harry Potter, *Magical DoReMi*, Studio Ghibli films, and *Avatar: The Last Airbender*. I love that series so much! It's the only one on the list that is not about witches, but its tone and character dynamics influenced Hooky a lot.

How did you develop the characters for the series?

The first time I drew Dani and Dorian was for Inktober 2014. If you're not familiar with Inktober, it's an artistic challenge created by the artist Jake Parker. You're supposed to make a drawing in ink every day in the month of October and post it online. I drew Dani and Dorian on October 20th and posted my art. I didn't know their names or their story yet, but I really enjoyed drawing them, so I did it again on October 24th. On November 15th, I posted a third drawing of them with a caption: "I grew quite fond of drawing these witch siblings . . . Maybe I'll draw a story about them one of these days." And here we are!

The main reason they're black and white is because it was an ink-drawing challenge. The simple design was also useful for WEBTOON, since you're supposed to draw an episode every week. I didn't follow that simplicity rule with the other characters, though. Monica and Nico have a lot more detail. In Monica's case, it makes sense to draw her as pretty and preppy, since she's a corny princess (at least in the beginning). Nico also has a lot of detail, but he's more chaotic.

Drawing fanart is a wonderful exercise, especially when we do it with our love for the original work as a base. Whether you want to draw the characters exactly the way I do (and this book will help you with that) or you want to give them your personal touch, just have fun and enjoy doing it.

Tell us about your art journey.

I've been drawing comics since I was a child. After high school, I studied at Escola Joso, a comic and visual arts school in Barcelona. It wasn't an easy decision. I felt like it was going to be hard to make a living from drawing comics, but I was passionate about it. In my third year of school, I discovered WEBTOON. They organized a worldwide contest to find new talent with a first prize of $30,000 and a contract to be a WEBTOON Original. I entered with those two cute witch siblings and posted my story in the platform. That's how Hooky started! I didn't win, but I kept drawing and posting the story because I was having so much fun. And there were readers following the story! After a month or two, I received an email from WEBTOON telling me they wanted Hooky to be part of the WEBTOON Originals!

What inspiration or advice would you give other artists?

Since drawing comics is hard work, don't try to use a perfect or detailed style if you're not sure you can finish it in the required time. This applies to WEBTOON and to comics in general. My case is a good example. My drawing style in school was different, with more detailed, realistic characters. One day, a teacher told me that my drawings looked "stiff" and that they lacked vitality and movement. The teacher pointed out the doodles I did mindlessly before doing my "real" drawing. She said that my simple, doodled style was more interesting and alive.

When I started drawing for WEBTOON, I used that same style because of how natural, easy, and quick it was for me. That was one of the keys that helped me meet the weekly deadlines. Little by little that style became more structured and detailed but still felt alive.

In short, my advice is that you shouldn't try to make your art perfect before starting your story—just use something that works for you, and it will become better with practice.

THE CHARACTERS

Meet the cast of Hooky!

DANIELA (DANI) WYTTE

Dani is extroverted and outgoing, which usually wins her fast friends, but she can also get into trouble when she finds herself leaping without looking. She excels at broom riding but she struggles with spells, and her magic is somewhat unpredictable—even dangerous—at times. As the older twin, Dani is very protective of her brother Dorian and goes out of her way to protect him. Early on, Dani is nearly burned at the stake after a misadventure goes particularly awry. This instills an even greater fear in her of becoming a witch.

COLOR PALETTE

HAIR COLOR	HAIR SHADOW/ EYES	SKIN	HAT	GOLD TRIM
#3E2B2E	#000000	#FFFFFF	#DB0A5B	#EFDBB2

Post Timeskip
Age: 16

After being tricked into believing Dorian is dead, Dani succumbs entirely to an evil spirit and the manipulation of her vengeful mother. This increases her magic ability exponentially but leaves her a hollow shell on a destructive rampage. It is only with the help of her friends and siblings that she's able to regain control of herself.

DORIAN WYTTE

Dorian does his best to follow his sister's lead, even when he knows the path it may lead them down could be a bumpy one. He's a talented witch and is more studious than Dani, meaning his spells tend to be more successful and less volatile. He cannot, however, ride brooms very well, and his shyness prevents him from making friends too easily.

COLOR PALETTE

HAIR COLOR	HAIR SHADOW/ EYES	SKIN	VEST
#3E2B2E	#000000	#FFFFFF	#5C4E63

Post Timeskip
Age: 16

Dorian goes missing after faking his own death, and it is eventually revealed that he was placed into a potion-induced coma thanks to a botched poisoning attempt. When he's found, he is being guarded by a dragon and is successfully revived with a healing potion.

DAMIEN WYTTE

Damien is the oldest Wytte child. When Damien was a child, he accidentally exposed his family as witches to the townsfolk, which provoked riots and terror around their home. As a result, his mother was nearly burned to death at the stake, prompting her to loathe all non-magic users. Even as a young child, Damien could see how dangerous and unstable his mother was becoming and fled his home to work in the castle for the royal family. There, he excelled in his new role as Prince William's personal butler—aided, perhaps, by the fact that he considered William to be the first friend he ever made who was able to see him for who and what he truly was.

COLOR PALETTE

HAIR COLOR/ SKIN	HAIR SHADOW/ EYES	CLOTHES
#FFFFFF	#7B798E	#221C35

Post Timeskip
Age: 23

Damien becomes a critical part of the rescue efforts for Dorian, who was in a magic-induced coma, rather than dying, thanks to Monica's potion. Thanks to him, and the efforts of Aisha, William, and Monica, they are eventually able to both restore Dani's memories and revive Dorian. In the process, however, Damien's feelings for Will continue to grow. Eventually, he and Will have to talk about their relationship and where it stands—despite Will's political marriage to Monica.

ANGELA WYTTE

Angela, mother to the Wytte children, was a gentle and caring woman who cherished and protected her family above all else. This changed when an accident resulted in her nearly being burned at the stake. Angela survived, but she was left severely burned and with most of her former gentleness reduced to ash. She became more steadily consumed with the idea of revenge against her attackers and all non-magic users. From this moment, Angela's life became a steady downward spiral into madness. She became manipulative, resentful, and bloodthirsty, seeming to have no qualms about using her children to get what she wanted. This, coupled with her charisma and passion, made for a powerful and dangerous combination. Angela was able to rally an army of witches and become a de facto symbol for magic users in her attempted revolution.

COLOR PALETTE

HAIR COLOR	HAIR SHADOW/ EYES	SKIN	BURN SCAR
#3E2B2E	#000000	#FFFFFF	#B46B7A

Angela is a slender woman with long black hair that sweeps down her back, usually in a braid. She wears some makeup that accentuates her eyelashes and lips. Her most striking facial feature is a large, mottled burn scar that covers about a quarter of her face, over her left eye. Angela almost always wears black or white blouses and skirts with black leggings.

MONICA

Monica is a confident (sometimes bossy) princess who believed herself to be a non-magic user for most of her life. She initially meets Dani and Dorian while they're studying with Master Pendragon, and their slowly growing friendship opens Monica's mind to the possibility that all witches may not be evil after all. She and Dorian spark a close relationship after a series of misunderstandings and false starts, and Monica eventually starts learning how to brew potions despite not being born a witch. As a princess, Monica wields a great deal of political power and is initially betrothed to William, even though she's not romantically interested in him. Instead, she finds herself falling for Dorian, even though she and William end up in a political marriage to share ruling duties for their respective kingdoms.

COLOR PALETTE

HAIR COLOR	HAIR SHADOW	DRESS	SKIN	EYES
#F4CDD4	#B07C83	#FDD26E	#FFFFFF	#AEA8A5

Post Timeskip
Age: 18

Despite not being a witch, Monica dedicates her time to learning potion-making and is instrumental to the eventual rescue of Dani and Dorian. Later, her engagement to Will culminates in a political marriage; however, the two remain platonic so she can pursue her interest in Dorian, while her husband can pursue his interest in Damien.

NICO

Nico was a sickly child who was saved from the brink of death by the magic of Pendragon. Unfortunately, his recovery did not go unnoticed by the neighbors who feared magic and witches. They promptly attacked his mother for being a "witch," despite her having no magical abilities whatsoever. Orphaned, Nico fell under the care of Pendragon, who raised him. But it wasn't exactly smooth sailing. Often caught between the world of magic users and non-magic users, Nico struggled to make friends until he met the Wyttes when they came to Pendragon for tutoring. His relationship with Dorian is tense at first—he begins to have feelings for Dani that cause him to act out. Despite his occasional boastfulness, Nico becomes a critical ally for the Wyttes as they discover more about the world of magic and their family. Eventually, Nico learns that he has a magical ability of his own: clairvoyance, which gives him the ability to see visions of the future that he can interpret and use to help his friends.

COLOR PALETTE

HAIR COLOR	HAIR SHADOW	SKIN	HEADBAND	LEOPARD PRINT	EYES
#F68D2E	#924C2E	#FFFFFF	#89813D	#F1C400	#EED484

Post Timeskip
Age: 18

Nico has a vision of Angela Wytte's coup against the king and queen, but his attempt to intervene lands him in the middle of a fight between Angela and Dani. To save him, Dani shrinks Nico down and pretends she teleported him to safety. But she is unable to transform him back to his regular size before Dorian's "death" and her possession, which lands him stuck in his minimized form indefinitely. Nico becomes something of a messenger between revolutionaries against the rule of witches and tries to help both Will and Aisha while also figuring out how to rescue Dani from her fate.

MARK EVANS

Mark is a non-magical commoner who was childhood friends with Nico; however, as they grew older, their relationship became more complicated and tense. Despite this, Mark still cares deeply for Nico and all his friends, including Dani, who initially had a crush on him. Mark's family runs the Evans Cafe, where Mark helps out, an experience that has given him more practical life skills—like driving and cooking—than many of his friends. He does, however, seem to lack book smarts.

COLOR PALETTE

HAIR COLOR	HAIR SHADOW/ EYEBROWS	EYES/ APRON	SKIN
#000000	#3E2B2E	#A0D1CA	#FFFFFF

Post Timeskip
Age: 20

Mark becomes increasingly close to Aisha over the timeskip years as they both help the resistance to the witches and aid in the recovery of both Dani and Dorian.

WILL

A non-magic user and prince, William was born into a life much more luxurious than a commoner. When he was a child, his father and Monica's father agreed to strengthen one another's kingdoms with an arranged marriage, meaning he and Monica have been betrothed since they were three years old. The two became close friends, thankfully—even after their fathers betrayed each other over a disagreement regarding the treatment of witches. Monica's father attempted to burn Angela Wytte at the stake, an event that would have dire consequences for everyone down the line. One of those consequences happened to be the arrival of Angela's son Damien to Will's kingdom. Damien became Will's friend and butler.

AGE: 17

COLOR PALETTE

HAIR COLOR	HAIR SHADOW/ EYEBROWS	EYES	SKIN
#B58150	#FFF8E6	#A2A468	#FFFFFF

Post Timeskip
Age: 20

Following the rescue of Dorian and Dani, Will takes up his late father's throne and goes through with his political marriage to Monica. The two of them use their influence to usher in a new era of understanding and peace between magic users and non-magic users while also allowing one another the freedom to pursue their own respective love interests. For Will, that happens to be Damien, who acts as his royal advisor.

AISHA

Despite her small frame, Aisha is older than most of her friends. This, coupled with her status as the princess of her kingdom, can make her come off as rude or stuck up in the beginning. She's extremely intelligent and level-headed, but she feels an immense sense of duty to her people and responsibilities. It's that sense of duty that prompts her to act in ways that are dangerous and risky—like when she decided to try and face down a dragon threatening her kingdom by herself, despite her lack of magical abilities.

COLOR PALETTE

HAIR COLOR	HAIR SHADOW	SKIN	TUNIC	JEWELRY	EYES
#714623	#3F2021	# E1B87F	#7C2529	#E0A526	#000000

Post Timeskip
Age: 20

Aisha became very close to Mark following Dorian's disappearance. She became one of the fighters against the rule of witches as she and her friends worked to recover the Wytte twins.

CHARACTER HEIGHT CHART

When developing a cast of characters for a story, it is good to map out how tall they are in relation to each other so you can keep consistency when drawing them together in various scenes.

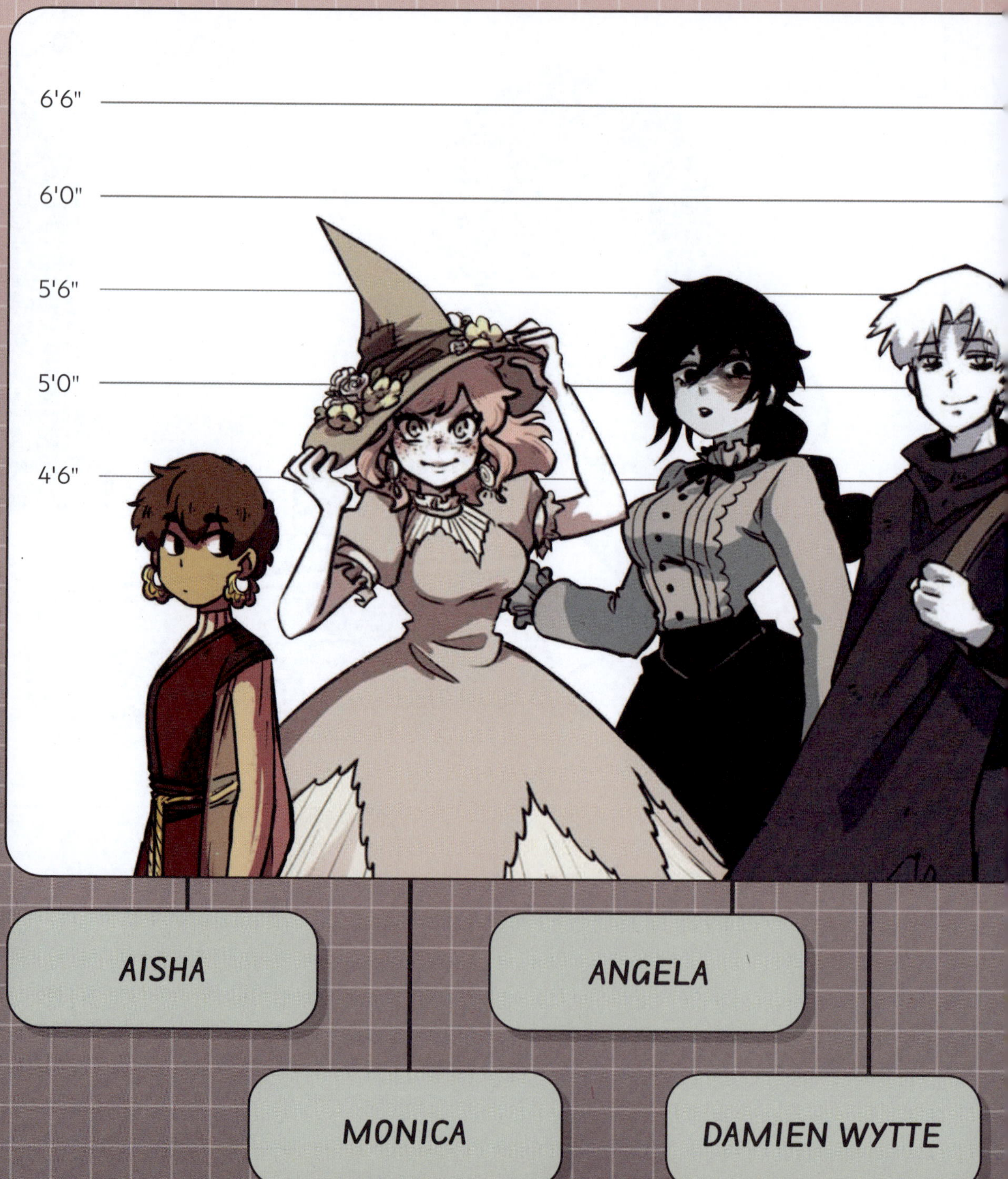

DANI WYTTE
NICO
DORIAN WYTTE
WILL
MARK EVANS

GETTING STARTED

Learn about the drawing and coloring process.

TOOLS & MATERIALS

Whether you are sketching on paper or drawing digitally, there are some basic tools that will help you on your artistic journey.

PENCILS

Graphite pencils come in various densities that help you achieve different shading techniques. The harder or denser the lead is, the lighter it will draw on paper. For a light shade, you can use a 2H pencil. An HB pencil will give you a medium shade, and for darker shades, you can use between 2B and 6B pencils. If you are a beginner artist, start with an HB pencil. Try different pencils and see which one works best for you.

ERASERS

When cleaning up your sketches, try using a good-quality rubber or vinyl eraser. You don't want something that will smudge your artwork as you are removing guidelines. A kneaded eraser is also a great tool and is a very pliable and versatile option that won't leave any dust or residue on your paper. You can mold the eraser into any shape to erase precisely.

PENS AND INKS

Fine-line markers come in different widths and are easy to use. Once you have finalized your sketches, it is great to go back and finish with a clean, sharp line. Make sure to use permanent ink markers so they won't smudge when adding color or erasing pencil lines. If you want variety in your pen strokes, try using a brush pen. The more pressure you use with a brush pen, the thicker the lines. Light pressure is perfect for very fine details.

PAPER

A sketchbook is a great tool for developing your art practice. They come in a variety of sizes and shapes, and you can bring one wherever you go. A good mixed-media sketchbook is a great place to start. If you are using paints or markers, choose a thicker paper so the wet media doesn't bleed through.

ADDING COLOR

Colored pencils are great for adding shading and depth to your drawings. Use sharp tips for detail work. Markers are perfect for adding large areas of color. Draw your strokes in quick succession to keep them smooth and blended. Add details or shading on top by letting your strokes dry first and then building up the color. Watercolor paints are also great medium to use to add color to your inked drawings.

DIGITAL TOOLS

Webcomics are created digitally, so it is great to familiarize yourself with digital drawing tools. There are many different drawing apps available at a low cost or even for free. Drawing tablets with pens can be used for digital drawing. There are many to choose from, so research and test out your options to find the right tablet for you.

Once the sketch is done, I finish the drawing with either Photoshop or Clip Studio Paint, depending on if I'm working on my desktop Wacom tablet or my iPad Pro. And I usually use the same brush: Kyle's Manga - Basic Rough.

DRAWING TIPS

There are different ways you can draw using traditional media, a combination of traditional and digital media, or digital media. Below are four different ways to draw. Try each of them out so you can decide what style works best for you.

Option 1: Traditional Media

Lightly sketch your drawing in pencil and then ink over it with a fine-tip pen or marker. Don't press too hard with your pencil or it might be harder to erase your marks later.

Option 2: Traditional Media + Light Box

Lightly sketch your drawing in pencil, and then ink over it on a clean sheet of paper. I use a light table to do this: Place your clean sheet of paper on top of the sketch. Lightly tape the sheets on top of a light box or light table. Then trace over the sketch using your inking tool. Your ink drawing will be completely clean, and you'll keep your original sketch intact! If you don't have access to a light table, tape your drawing and clean paper on a window and follow the same directions.

Option 3: Traditional Media + Digital Media

Lightly sketch your drawing in blue pencil and ink over it with your pen as you normally would. Scan the drawing to your computer and remove the blue marks digitally.

Option 4: Digital Media

If you work digitally with a graphics tablet, simply sketch your drawing on one layer and ink your drawing on a separate layer. This is what I do today—there is no denying it saves a lot of time.

HEAD SHAPES

It's important to have a solid grasp of the basics when drawing characters. When you start to learn basic human anatomy and how it works, it is one of the easiest ways to learn how to draw a three-dimensional figure on a two-dimensional space.

BASIC PROPORTIONS: KID FACES

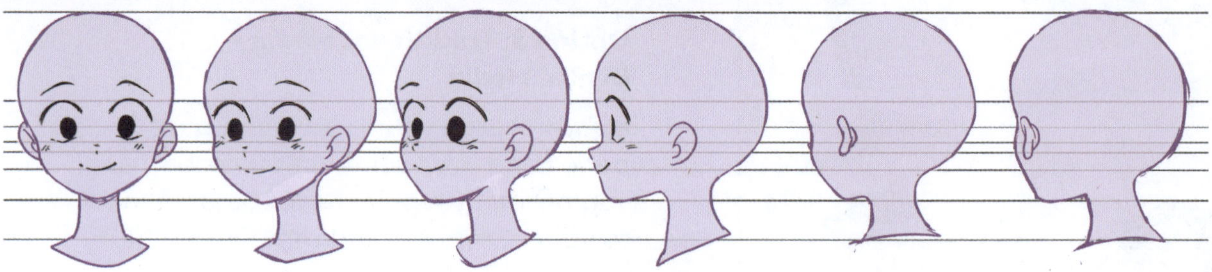

Dani and Dorian have the same face, so this could be either of them.

- BIG FOREHEAD
- BIG EYES
- SMALL NOSE CLOSE TO THE MOUTH
- SOFT JAWLINE
- THIN NECK

BASIC PROPORTIONS: TEEN FACES

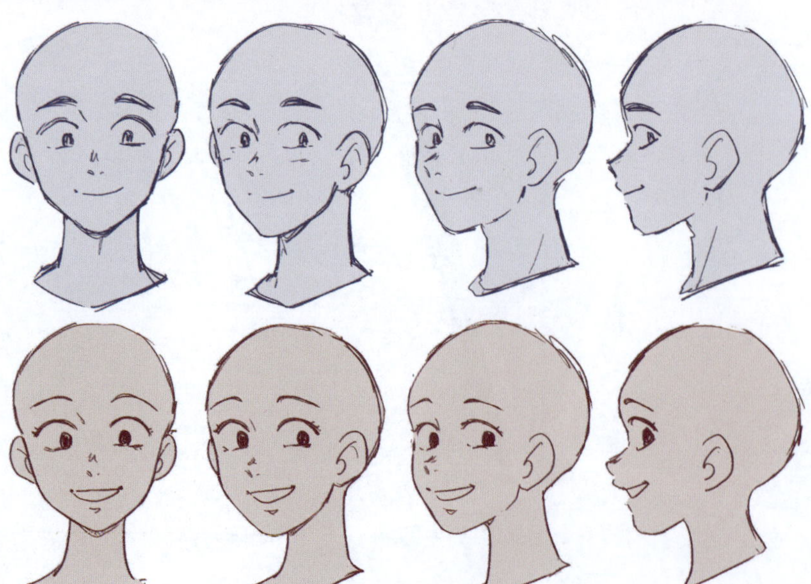

To age up Dorian, Dani, Monica, and Nico, I slightly changed their face proportions.

The face gets longer, the nose bigger, the neck thicker, and the eyes smaller. The eyes and nose become more separated.

I use fewer round lines as they age, especially in boys.

Once you have the basic proportions down, don't be afraid to play with different face shapes and angles!

I don't always pay attention to drawing the perfect ratio. I prefer to focus on movement and interesting expressions.

EXPRESSIONS

Expressions are important because they help convey a character's mood and motivation while also contributing to the action of each scene. Below are some common expressions seen in Hooky.

ANGRY

ASTONISHED

NERVOUS

FOCUSED

CHEERFUL

CONFIDENT

SUSPICIOUS

DETERMINED

AFRAID

SHY

SHOCKED

FUMING

HAPPY

JOYFUL

DISTRESSED

EYES

As a manga artist, I have always been in danger of falling into "same face syndrome." It's a common thing among artists, but those of us who draw comics, manga, and webcomics should especially do what we can to avoid it! The more different the characters are from each other, the better—and the eyes are a good place to start. As you can see, the eyes of the Hooky characters are very different from each other.

DORIAN

DANI

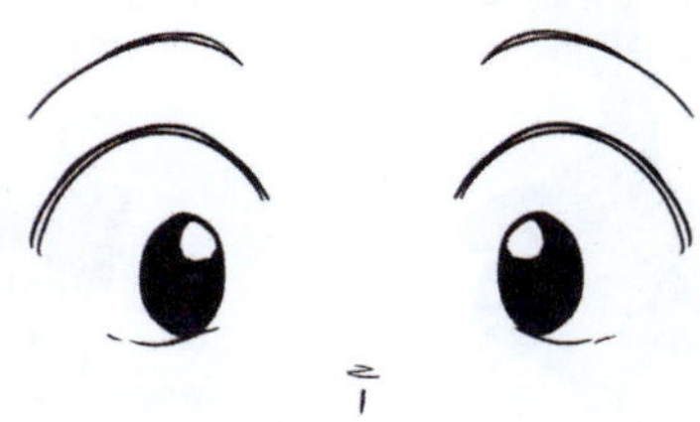

DAMIEN

MONICA

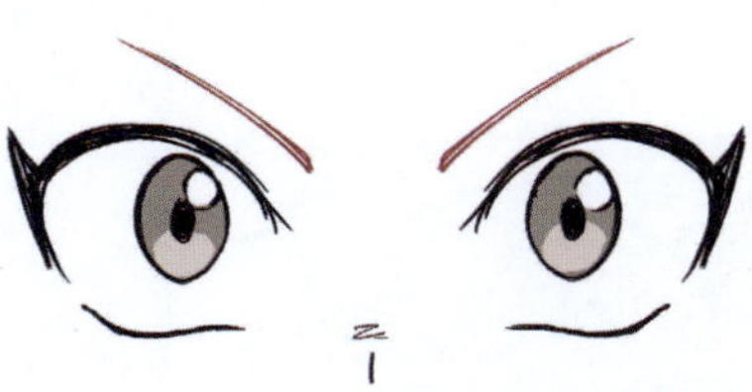

NICO

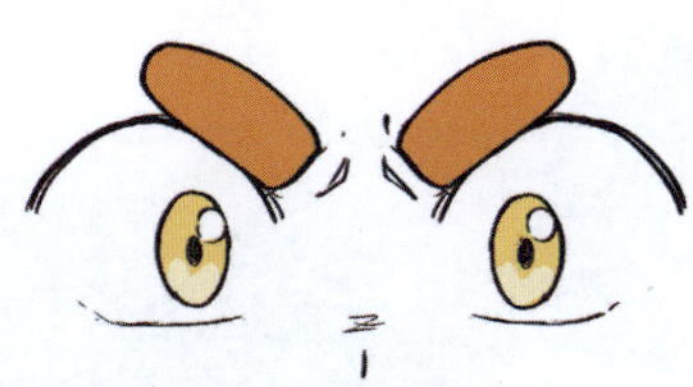

MARK EVANS

AISHA

WILL

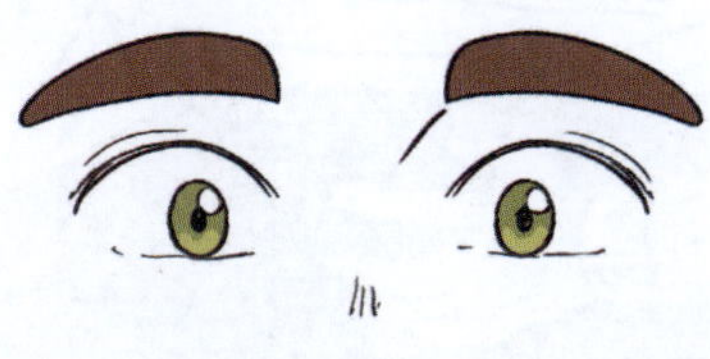

ANGELA

AGING UP A CHARACTER

Hooky is a coming-of-age story, so of course the characters had to grow up! And it was really fast! Because there was a three-year timeskip, I had the opportunity to make new designs for everyone. It was so much fun! To be fair, I didn't change their styles (except for Dani during her "dark era"). Basically, all the characters are taller (especially Dani and Dorian) and have more mature features and personalities. Damien didn't grow a bit though!

12-13 YEARS OLD

16-17 YEARS OLD

DANI & DORIAN

MONICA & DORIAN

NICO

BODY SHAPES & MOVEMENT

Since my art style is influenced by manga, I tend to draw my characters with bigger heads, longer legs, and shorter torsos instead of in more "realistic" proportions. My characters, even if they're adults, have more childlike or doll proportions and soft lines, so that's why the Hooky art style feels cute.

Body height is measured in head size, which means each section of the body is roughly the same size as the head. This kid body is about six heads tall, while the teen body is about seven heads tall—although the male teen body is a tiny bit taller than the female teen body.

BASIC SHAPE: KID BODY

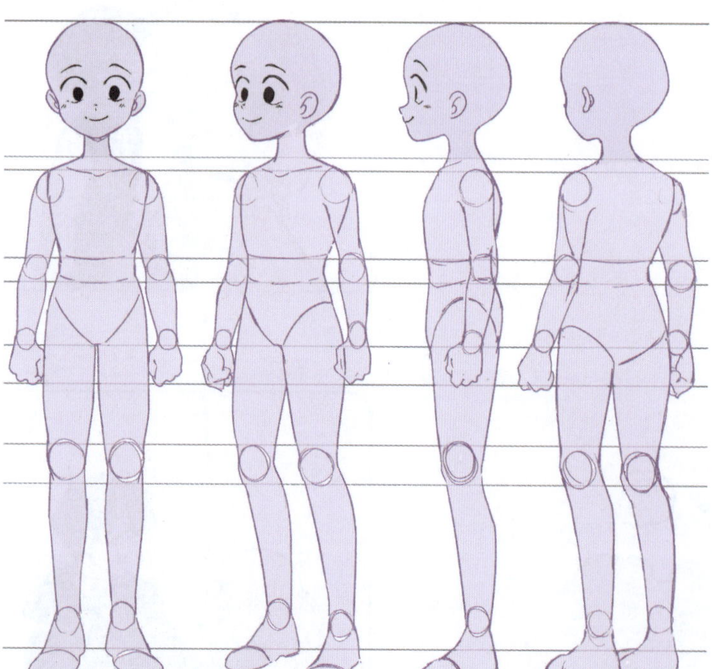

BASIC SHAPE: TEEN BODY

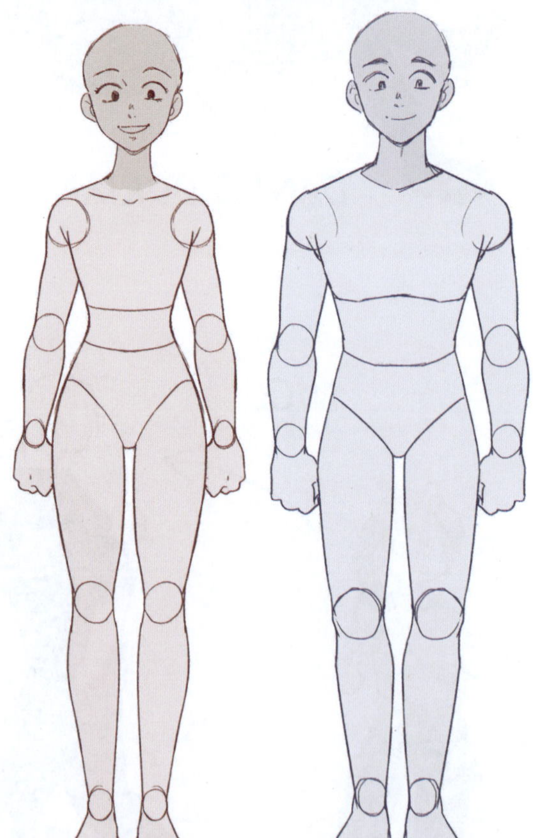

Knowing body proportions is important. But, to me, the "flow" of a drawing is more essential. To ensure my characters feel alive, I base the whole drawing on the first thumbnail, which I sketch without minding proportions, while imagining my characters' movements and reactions.

A

Thumbnail Sketch (A). This rough, tiny sketch helps me work out the scene and movement of the characters.

B

Rough Sketch (B). Here I work out the proportions and start to create a clearer image.

C

Line Art (C). Usually, I go straight to the line art after my rough sketch. If needed, I add more details to complete the scene.

D

Final Color (D). Here is where my drawing and webcomic scene come to life!

CLOTHING & ACCESSORIES

CHARACTER COLORS & THEMES

The Wytte Twins

All the witches in Hooky wear black, and Dani and Dorian are no exception. They also wear elegant and formal clothes, which are symbolic of their upper-class background and education. As the story progresses, Dani starts wearing more relaxed clothes. In the end, she and Dorian still wear similar outfits, but they're no longer all black, and Dorian is slightly more formal. He tends to wear more blue, and Dani prefers red. They both share purple, though—after all, blue + red = purple!

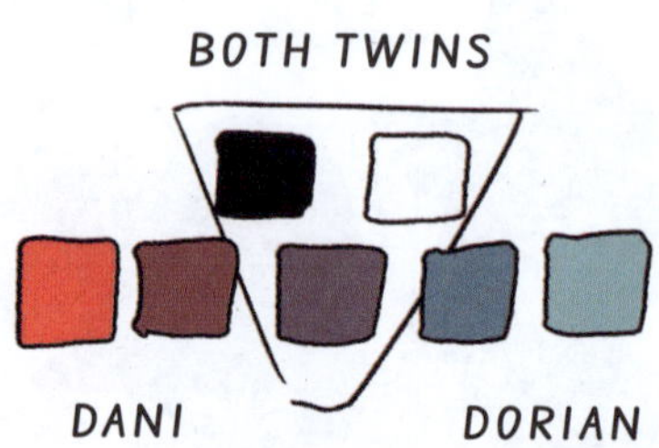

Princess Monica

Monica is a princess, and she loves dresses. As a child, she wears long, full dresses with ribbons and soft colors like pink. Once she leaves the castle to find her fiancé, her dresses become shorter with fewer details. She also stops wearing pink and starts wearing yellow, mustard, and orange, which reflect her bubbly and energetic personality.

Nico

Nico has a ragged style with torn clothes, headscarves, earrings, wild prints, and bandages everywhere. He often resembles a pirate! Nico was raised by Pendragon rather ineptly, without financial stability. His color is green, which makes his orange hair stand out, but he also wears browns and earth tones to highlight his street-like character. When he grows up, he is no longer dirty but still retains a rebellious style.

MATCHING OUTFITS

A

B

From the beginning of the series, I have matched outfits between characters. Dani and Dorian's matching outfits make it more obvious that they're twins and have a close relationship (A).

When Dani and Dorian are in conflict with each other, I highlight the distance through the clothes they wear (B).

Monica and Dani match as the two queens.

Mark and Monica match at the Castle Ball, since they are dancing partners.

Will and Damien match as the king and his witch counsel.

When the three siblings are together, they wear matching outfits—or at least when they go to family reunions!

CHANGING ART STYLES

When starting a new series, my advice is to use an art style that is comfortable and quick. Don't try to be a perfectionist or use a detailed style if you're not sure you can finish it in the required time. This advice applies to WEBTOON and comics in general.

When I started drawing Hooky for WEBTOON, I used a more casual art style because it came more naturally to me. This was key in helping me meet my deadlines. Over time, this style has become more structured and detailed.

In short, don't try to make your art perfect before starting your story; just use something that works for you, and it will become better with practice.

Episodes 1–39	Episodes 40–50	Now

DANI		

DORIAN		

NICO		

MONICA		

Experiment with your style and be open to changing it over time. It's common for art styles to grow and evolve, and it will keep your audience engaged and interested to see how the art changes with maturing characters and dynamic storylines.

COLOR TIPS

Many vignettes are needed for each webcomic episode on WEBTOON. To help save time, I limit my color palettes as much as possible. Below are some tricks I use to help save time when applying color.

A

For a simple background, I will alternate between two or three flat colors to add more interest to the composition (A).

B

C

To make things easy, I will use the same colors in the background that already exist in the scene—like in the umbrella (B) and planter (C).

D

With the limited background color palette, you can easily move from scene to scene, adjusting for the action and story as you go (D).

Shadows add depth and drama to a scene. I apply shadows using digital tools by creating a shadow layer and then duplicating it. I darken the second layer overall in the same color scheme of my base color. With the Gradient Tool set to radial, I delete the areas where I don't want the shadow to appear.

To create bold outlines in a scene, use black outlines (A). To add more definition to darker areas in a scene, change black lines to color lines that match the palette (B).

A

B

USING COLOR TO EMPHASIZE EMOTIONS

Color is an effective way to quickly communicate aspects of a scene, particularly emotion. These examples show how I generally use color in my scenes.

Red has an energy that can communicate passion, pain, rage, anger, and violence.

Pink is ideal for showing love, tenderness, softness, and calm.

Green often represents nature, but it can be effective in showing toxic, disgusting, or creepy things.

Blue can convey sadness, depression, or disappointment.

DRAWING STEP BY STEP

Learn to draw the characters of Hooky!

LEARN TO DRAW YOUNGER DANI

My drawing process starts with a series of rough sketches. From there, I go to ink and then finalize the details before moving to color. At the color stage, I apply flat areas of color. Then I polish the drawing by adding shadows, highlights, and any other final details. You can replicate my method or use any method that works for you!

1

I treat my initial sketches as one step and continue to adjust the details until I am happy with my drawing. Then I use the final sketch as a guide.

2

Using my sketch lines as a guide, I ink my drawing in black (step 2) and then erase any old sketch lines (step 3).

3

I add flat color to my inked drawing (step 4) and then add depth and dimension with highlights and shadows (step 5).

4

5

I like creating voluminous hairstyles drawing inspiration from '90s anime. It's especially noticeable in the bangs.

LEARN TO DRAW YOUNGER DORIAN

Young Dani and Dorian share similar features, including rounded faces and large eyes. They are, for me, the easiest to draw because their round, adorable shapes come naturally to me—I love drawing cute things—and because their features are similar.

Young Dani and Dorian have large, round, and cheerful eyes.

1

Begin by sketching Dorian's face and neck.

2

Start the inking process (step 2) and clean up your artwork by erasing old sketch lines (step 3).

3

4

5

Add flat color to your inked drawing (step 4) and then add depth and dimension with highlights and shadows (step 5).

LEARN TO DRAW OLDER DANI

In the final third of the story, Dani and Dorian are teenagers. Designing older versions of their characters was a fun challenge. Although they are still young (with big eyes, smooth skin, and round faces), both of their faces have lengthened a bit more, and the eyes don't take up as much of the face.

1

Begin with your series of sketches.

2

Ink over your sketch (step 2) and erase any old sketch lines now or after you've added your first round of flat color (step 3). Add shadows and highlights as desired (step 4).

3

4

Lengthening Dani's hair, narrowing her jaw, and changing her outfit and accessories gives her an older look. As the twins get older, they start to look less alike.

LEARN TO DRAW OLDER DORIAN

Older Dorian has slightly smaller eyes and thicker eyebrows and, like Dani, has a more angular jaw and a longer, narrower face.

1

Begin with your first sketches.

Both Dani and Dorian's noses are larger. Dorian's nose is farther from his eyes.

2

Ink over your sketch (step 2) and erase any old sketch lines now or after you've added your first round of flat color (step 3).

3

4

Add shadows and highlights as desired (step 4).

Even though they are older, Dani and Dorian sometimes wear clothes that match in color and basic style.

LEARN TO DRAW DANI & DORIAN

For body poses, I start with a very rough sketch and then begin to accentuate the anatomy and fill in the details as I go.

1

Start with a rough pose.

2

Begin filling out the body shapes and refining the details.

3

Ink your drawing and move to the color stage.

COMIC COLORING STYLE

4

When adding shadows to art with flat color, I select lilac, pink, or blue (depending on the scene) and, in Multiply mode, add a layer that uses one color for all shadow work, as shown here.

ILLUSTRATION COLORING STYLE

When I have more time and want to add more color, I use a more detailed style and add shadows, highlights, blushing cheeks, and outlines, all of which make the illustration softer.

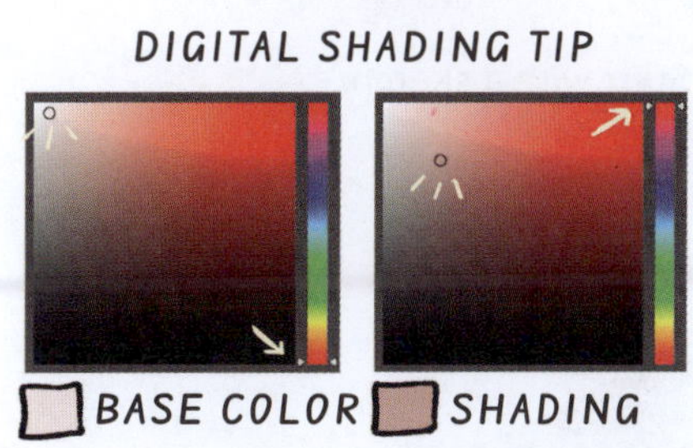

LEARN TO DRAW DAMIEN WYTTE: HEAD

Damien's features are sharp and angular. His face always carries a rather intense and morose expression as well.

1

Start with a sketch.

2

Continue to follow the same steps as you did for the previous characters to complete your drawing.

3

4

Damien's hair falls in loose waves in front of his forehead.

LEARN TO DRAW DAMIEN WYTTE: BODY

Damien's posture is usually tense and stiff. His body communicates his mood with arms crossed and feet planted in a leaning stance.

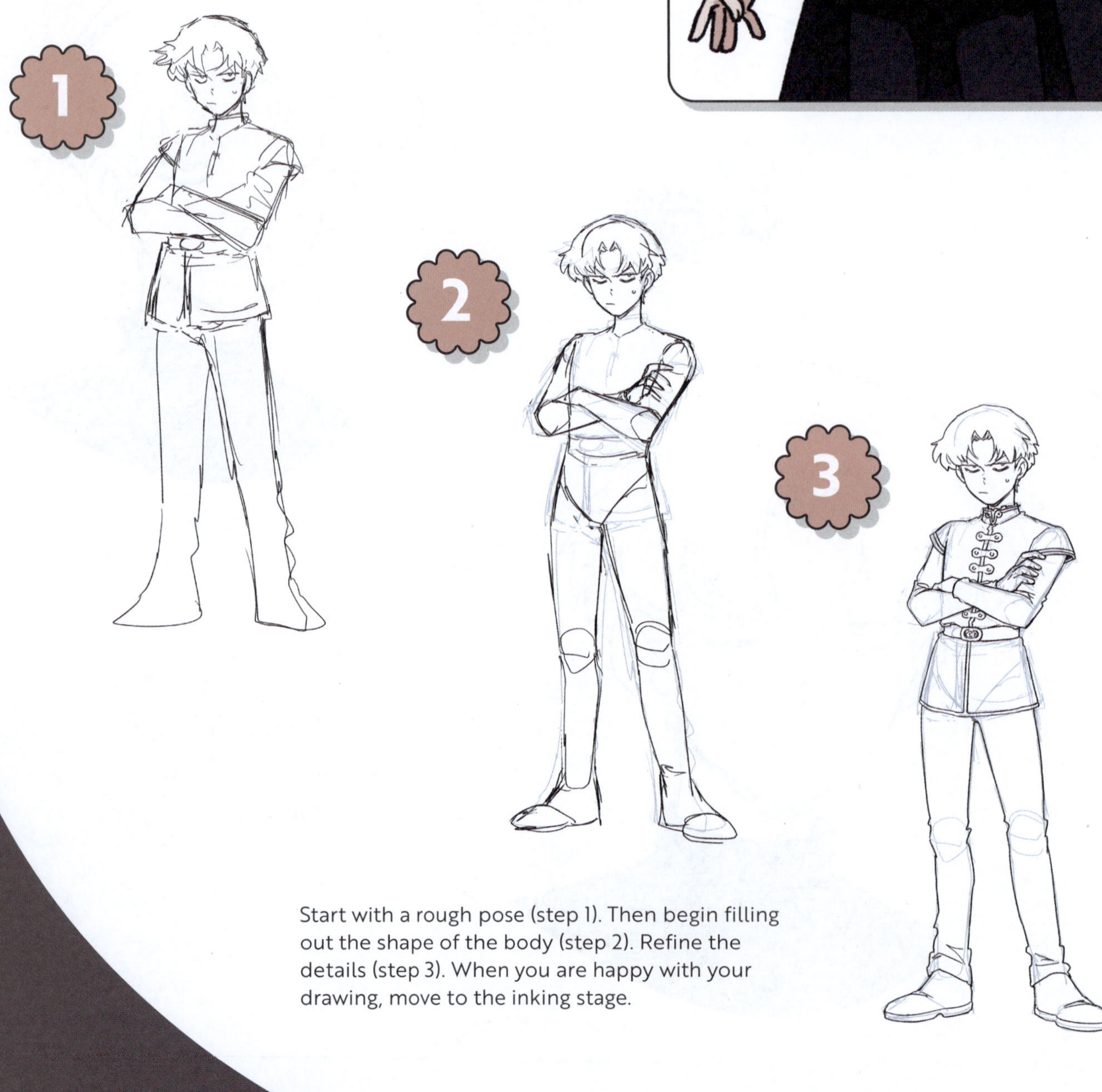

Start with a rough pose (step 1). Then begin filling out the shape of the body (step 2). Refine the details (step 3). When you are happy with your drawing, move to the inking stage.

4

Ink your drawing (step 4) and fill in the shape with flat color (step 5). Finish your drawing by adding highlights and shadows (step 6).

5

6

Drawing tiny, narrow eyes gives Damien an unsettled and jaded look, which is the opposite of the cheerful and happy look in Dani's and Dorian's eyes.

LEARN TO DRAW MONICA: HEAD

Monica is pretty, feminine, and fierce. I love to draw her with that defiant smile and almost feline look. Unlike Dani and Dorian who have round, simple eyes, Monica has large almond-shaped eyes with a "cat-eye" eyeliner look. I love drawing her long, voluminous hair.

1

Start with a sketch.

Ink over your sketch (step 2) and erase any old sketch lines now (step 3) or after you've added your first round of flat color (step 4).

Complete your drawing by adding shadows and highlights (step 5).

2

3

4

5

Monica has freckles that dot the bridge of her nose and part of her cheeks.

LEARN TO DRAW MONICA: BODY

Monica is an expressive character who experiences a range of emotions through her facial expressions and body postures.

Start with a rough pose (step 1). Then begin filling out the shape of the body (step 2). Refine the details (step 3).

4

When you are happy with your drawing, move to the inking stage (step 4). Add flat color (step 5) and complete the drawing by adding shadows and highlights (step 6).

5

6

Monica's feminine look includes ruffles, flowers, and lace accents.

LEARN TO DRAW NICO: HEAD

Nico's face has straighter lines and sharper features. His hair is a combination of points and tips. All this, together with his thick eyebrows, helps him have a "rough" appearance that matches his thuglike personality.

1

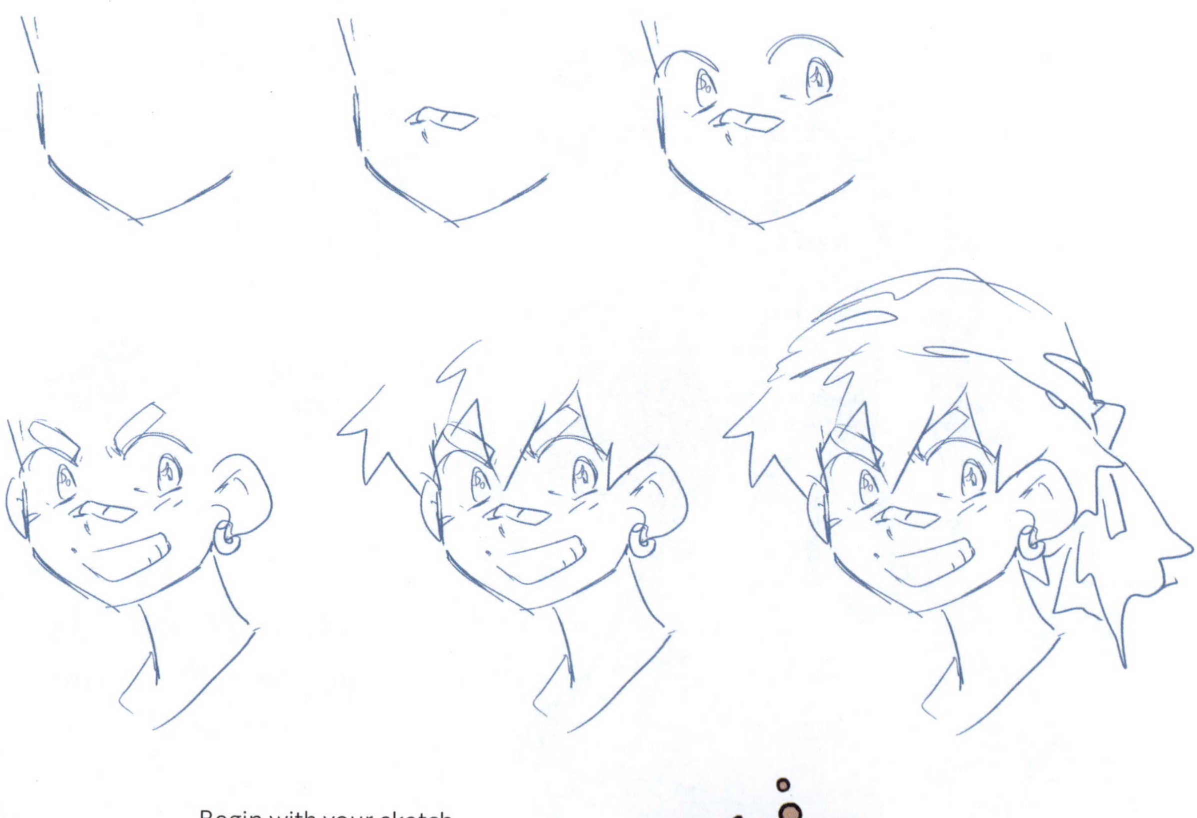

Begin with your sketch.

Move to inking.

Apply flat color to your drawing (step 3) and add highlights and shadows to complete the drawing (step 4).

Nico's angular features and furrowed brows give his face a mischievous appearance.

LEARN TO DRAW NICO: BODY

Nico is confident and cocky, and this often shows in his body posture. Here, he has a hand behind his head and is holding up a peace sign while striking a casual pose of feet crossed.

1

2

3

Start with a rough pose (step 1). Then begin filling out the shape of the body (step 2). Refine the details (step 3).

When you are happy with your drawing, move to the inking stage (step 4). Add flat color (step 5) and complete the drawing by adding shadows and highlights (step 6).

4

5

6

Nico's clothes have a patchwork quality to them that suggest he's a little rough around the edges. His bandanna, earrings, and bracelet add to his overall style.

LEARN TO DRAW MARK EVANS: HEAD

Mark has traditionally masculine features, including a pointed jawline and a muscular neck.

1

Begin with a sketch.

When you are happy with your drawing, move to the inking stage (step 2) and finesse the details (step 3). Add flat color (step 4) and complete the drawing by adding shadows and highlights (step 5).

2

3

4

5

Mark wears a shirt over a sleeveless tank and has a collar that flares out.

LEARN TO DRAW MARK EVANS: BODY

Mark Evans has a casual disposition, which matches his relaxed posture in this pose. What he lacks in book smarts he makes up for as a loyal friend.

Start with a rough pose (step 1). Then begin filling out the shape of the body (step 2). Refine the details (step 3).

4

When you are happy with your drawing, move to the inking stage (step 4). Add flat color (step 5) and complete the drawing by adding shadows and highlights (step 6).

5

Mark's apron from the cafe has a cup of coffee on it.

6

LEARN TO DRAW WILL: HEAD

Will has complicated relationships in this series, from his family to Angela to Damien. His many facial expressions reflect what he is going through at any given time.

1

Begin with a sketch.

2

When you are happy with your drawing, move to inking.

3

Apply flat color (step 3) and then add highlights and shadows to finish your drawing (step 4).

4

For a more intense facial expression, draw Will's eyebrows pointing downward.

LEARN TO DRAW WILL: BODY

Will's basic anatomy is similar to Mark Evans's. Once you master one character, you can apply those same skills to draw the other character.

Start with a rough pose (step 1). Then begin filling out the shape of the body (step 2). Refine the details (step 3).

4

When you are happy with your drawing, move to the inking stage (step 4). Add flat color (step 5) and complete the drawing by adding shadows and highlights (step 6).

5

6

Will can also be in a relaxed state, which shows here in his face with a wide smile and a casual body pose with hands in his pockets.

LEARN TO DRAW AISHA

Aisha has moxie and sass. She isn't afraid of much, and it shows when she jumps in to help her friends. Your drawings of Aisha should reflect her can-do attitude.

1

Follow the steps from the previous projects to draw Aisha's head and face.

2

3

4

Follow the steps from the previous projects to draw Aisha's full-body pose.

LEARN TO DRAW CARLO

Carlo—the apple of our eyes! And what eyes! Yes, Carlo is a dragon frog, but I try to make him look like a cuddly stuffed animal with circles and rounded shapes. That is, except for his batlike wings and pointed tail—there had to be something threatening about him, the poor thing. After all, he is a dragon!

1

Begin by sketching Carlo's face and body.

Start the inking process (step 2) and clean up your artwork by erasing old sketch lines (step 3).

2

3

Add flat color to your inked drawing (step 4) and then add depth and dimension with highlights and shadows (step 5).

4

5

INTRODUCTION TO WEBCOMICS

Turn your drawings into stories!

INTRODUCTION TO PUBLISHING ON WEBTOON

WEBTOON introduced a new way to create stories for anyone who has a story to tell. If you want to publish your own webcomic, your story can start with CANVAS, WEBTOON's self-publishing platform.

Posting on CANVAS means that you, as a creator, have control over all aspects of your story and can use the platform to build a unique audience thanks to the thousands of readers that visit the platform daily.

Some of WEBTOON's most popular titles began on WEBTOON CANVAS. WEBTOON Originals are stories that are developed for the platform.

Unlike traditional comics, which are meant to be read in a print format, WEBTOON is a mobile-based platform, so the content has been formatted to be read vertically.

Through the vertical format, reading a WEBTOON series is meant to feel like a cinematic experience since the reader can see only one panel at a time instead of the entire page like in a traditional print comic.

If you have a story to tell and want to create your own webcomic, it takes planning.

DEVELOP YOUR CHARACTERS

Creating believable characters is one of the most important tasks for any creator. When developing a character for your story, consider these parameters in order to have a good understanding of who they are; this will ground the character in your story and make them seem more believable to the reader:

- What is their role in the story?
- What is this character's intended arc? A character arc is usually the internal journey a character goes through over the course of the story.
- What are their strengths and weaknesses?
- What relationships do they have with other characters in the story?
- What is their motivation?

CREATE CHARACTER SHEETS

- Character Designs / Physical
- Characteristics / Color Palette
- Motivations (Wants vs. Needs)
- Mannerisms, Perks, and Flaws
- Circle of Being (Backstory)

PLAN YOUR STORY

What is the setting?

This is the location of the action that includes time and place (when and where).

What is the overall plot of your story?

The plot is the actual story. A plot should have a beginning, middle, and end, with a clear conflict and resolution:

- Conflict is usually a problem the plot is intended to resolve, and without conflict, there's no story to tell.
- Resolution is the solution to the main conflict of the story. It's important to make sure the resolution feels earned by wrapping up the main story conflict, character arcs, and setting.

THUMBNAILS

This is when you plan out your panels based on your story. Thumbnails are intended to be very loose, simple drawings that will help you have an understanding of how the episode will be structured. Storyboarding an episode can help creators plan scenes and sequences with pacing, clarity, and readability in mind for readers.

SKETCHES

Once you've created your rough thumbnails, you're ready to start sketching your characters and backgrounds. This is also the stage when creators plan out the placement of their speech bubbles.

INKING

Inking is the process of cleaning up your lines to create a more polished look.

COLORING & FINALIZING

Add color, speech bubbles, special effects, and lettering.

ILLUSTRATING A SCENE

My process for illustrating a scene is quite detailed and includes experimenting with composition, color, background, and details. Here I walk through a basic outline of how I render a scene from start to finish.

STEP ONE: THUMBNAIL SKETCH

All my illustrations start with a thumbnail sketch to figure out if the characters, action, and composition I'm imagining work together in a scene.

STEP TWO: ROUGH IN THE DETAILS

Next, I draw a rough sketch, but as you can see, the drawing is starting to take shape.

STEP THREE: REFINE THE DETAILS

If you don't know how to draw an item from your imagination, it's helpful to look at references. I am terrible at drawing vehicles, so I had to look for references of vans. My van does not have realistic proportions, but the parts are in their right places.

Now I begin adding in the details while refining the piece and cleaning up old sketch lines.

STEP FOUR: ROUGH IN COLOR

When my line art is complete, I start adding flat color. Here I experiment with different hues, shades, and tones until I find the color combinations I like.

STEP FIVE: MAKE ADJUSTMENTS

I wasn't going to include a background in this piece—I really wanted to highlight the characters on their own, but it wasn't coming together. So I opt to add an open frame, like a comic strip, and draw a background. I think it gives the illustration more of a storybook feel, which suits Hooky quite well—and it looks cute.

STEP SIX: REFINE THE COLOR

I continue to add color to the piece and realize that it will look much more defined if I add outlines, which helps better separate the elements in such a detailed piece.

Details like these light-colored flowers would get lost in this piece if they weren't outlined.

STEP SEVEN: FINISHING TOUCHES

Now I add shadows and highlights (see below), a little blush here, a little freckle there, and a sparkle in the eyes. I also experiment with hue, saturation, and gradient until the colors feel beautiful and harmonious. And we're done!

My shading and highlights are very simple. I usually do a single level of shading and highlights on parts I consider to be essential—in this case, the van headlights, the cauldron on top of the van, and a few other small areas. For the shadows, I darken the base color a little at a time.

ABOUT THE CREATOR

Míriam Bonastre Tur is the *New York Times* bestselling author of Hooky and the creator of the WEBTOON series Marionetta. She was born in a small town near Barcelona and doodled on any smooth surface before even learning to walk. She studied comics at the Escola Joso Center for Comics and Visual Arts in Barcelona. She has drawn many zines and collaborative comics in Spanish, and now works as a character designer in the animation field. She lives in Spain.

I would love for you to share your drawings! Feel free to tag me on Instagram and X: @miriambonastre